I dedicate this b
Butterflies Dementia Support a

To Julie Brown and the volunteers who work
tirelessly helping people and their carers to cope
with Dementia and other disabilities both mentally
and physically, touching so many peoples lives.

Butterflies
Dementia Support and Activities Group

First published in the United Kingdom by Arc Publishing and Print 2022

Text copyright © Susan Morgan 2022

ISBN: 978-1-906722-88-3

Index

Blank Spaces

I had memories
shared with so many
time was a friend
I have been blessed.
Inside this space
thoughts are fleeting
as my mind struggles
another door slams shut
logic and sense lost.
More blank spaces
and confusion.
I was articulate, now I forget
more than I remember
as this illness
takes the folds of my mind
and fragments them.
Please let me keep
what is worth keeping,
let it be more
than a photograph
of strangers, and
when everything is grey, I pray
Let me remember
Love.

A Hard man

And his ways are ways of gentleness
now the years are behind him
but his ways were different then
 a giant with hands like shovels
tall and strong afraid of no one.
Gambling was in his blood
his mind sharp as a needle, always in control
there were no hugs or kisses, yet
we were loved and provided for.
With a short fuse
violence came easy to a hard man
his angry cursing would shake the room.
He is different now, small and fragile
dependent on strangers
time has tamed him
and his ways are ways of gentleness.

A Praise Poem for Retirement

I write in praise of retirement
the open door of opportunity
a lie in bed time for planning
without the alarm clock.

I write in praise of pleasing myself
choosing companions and pastimes
grasping the true meaning of freedom
spreading my wings.

I write in praise of the drifting
flowing softness, without structure.
life worn smooth like a stone
and at last, appreciating its beauty.

I write in praise of the inevitable
graying hair, wrinkles, warts
and elastic waistbands.
Proud to say, this is me.

I write in praise of contentment
happy in my own skin
to look back on life and say
Up yours!

A Praise Poem for the Sun

I write in praise of the sun
controlling the seasons and time
waking the earth, yawning and stretching
into life as it spreads it's warmth, defrosting
Winter into Spring.
The beauty of its light
a dazzling intensity that fills every room
as shadows and shade creep silently
chasing darkness into submission.
The comfort of its heat
lifting spirits into a state of euphoria
soon, turning into a blistering inferno
burning the earth to a pie crust.

The Fickle Wind

You're always welcome as a cool Summer breeze
whispering sweet nothings and flirting with the trees
singing through the grasses, blowing kisses to the vine
drying all the washing as it dances on the line.
Why chase away the blue skies to bring raincloud?
scattering petals when flowers bloom, standing proud
fickle wind of change with your anger and bluster
shaking laden branches as scented blossoms cluster.
Gathering memento, you whistle and groan
changing direction, you chill to the bone
scattering leaves in a merry dance
turning them gold from green in a glance.
Indiscriminately you bluster and blow
gradually wilder and stronger although
you don't scare me; you'll soon blow yourself out
like a candle, and quickly disappear no doubt.

The Alphabet Garden

As the sun sets
Bringing the garden cool release
Casting shadows across the soil
Daylight comes to an end
Evening brings solitude and peace.
Fungi flourish where no one passes
Grasshoppers chirp as they
Hide in the grasses
Ivy climbs, covering the wall
Jerusalem Artichokes growing tall.
Kidney beans curl around the cane
Lettuces sit pretty under a frame
Manure is piled behind the shed
Next to the roses that grow in a bed.
Organic
Potatoes, parsnips and peas
Queue in orderly rows if you please,
Resting upright against the shed
Stand the fork, the hoe and the spade
Tools essential for a gardener's trade.
Under the shade of the apple tree
Violets and buttercups wait for the bee,
Webs are spun in the twilight hour
Xerophytes sticky tendrils run,
Yellow petals of the
Zinnia reflects the setting sun.

The Poppy Field

Just by chance, I turned to look
Such joy! I gazed in awe
A hundred thousand poppies
A hundred thousand more.

Blood red on the horizon
A blazing field I saw
This patchwork quilt of colour
A hundred thousand more.

This feast of fiery poppies
I'm sure weren't there before
Swaying in the gentle breeze
A hundred thousand more.

If I could paint this picture
Sheer pleasure to restore
Stand proud in all their glory
A hundred thousand more.

Man shamed this crimson beauty
On the bloody field of war!
A hundred thousand poppies
A hundred thousand more.

D.I.Y.
A Monologue

Now don't get me wrong, I love him to bits, my husband and partner in life,
He's so kind and thoughtful and funny, we rarely have any strife.
Except on the odd occasion........
When we both have to laugh or we'd cry,
And that's when he get's out his tools, and starts with his D.I.Y.

We decided we'd have a new carpet, best quality, ooh it was posh,
Hard at it all day, he fitted it down
He said it would save us some dosh.
However, the door wouldn't open....
So in a flash, he took out his plane,
And taking the door off its hinges
Started planeing like someone insane.
He must have been at it ten minutes,
There were shavings all over the floor
He hung the door back on its hinges
Then my blood pressure started to soar,
On the top of the door was a two-inch gap...
And we still couldn't open the door!!

Like the time I bought flat-pack cupboards,
Said he needed an A-level course,
The bits didn't fit, he shouted a bit,
It very near caused a divorce!
Then when he tried to fit them,
It wouldn't be easy, I could tell,
That's when he drilled through the water –pipe,
And flooded the kitchen as well!

He then decorated the bedroom,
The wallpaper cost a few bob
And apart from the pasto on the carpet,
God bless him, he'd done a grand job.
But then, after closer inspection,
My smile soon turned into a frown,
The wallpaper pattern looked lovely
But the border was on upside down!!
Now I dread if something needs mending,
But I know common sense will prevail,
My Peter-Pan turns into Danger Man
When he goes for a hammer and nail.
So now after years of mishaps,
My protest he still over rules,
And I smile...something's bound to go wrong
When my D.I.Y. man gets out his tools!

What does the heart weigh?

What does the heart weigh?
More than the touch of a frail hand
or the enigmatic smile that still lights up a room
more than the frightened child behind
those tired eyes that have lost their sparkle?
Under the tender pressure of age
days spent in slippers
with buttons done up wrong, when
night becomes day, and bed
the only memory of consolation
a tragic thread of comfort.
We share blood, what does it matter?
deep in mirrors
you see a stranger.

Your Old Wedding Ring

Do you know you wear your lifetime on your hand?
A circle of love in your gold wedding band
Cast your mind back to that day in your life
In a cloud of confetti, you became a new wife.
A symbol of marriage for the world to see
A lifetime of commitment worn confidently
Stoic years with someone you can always depend
Like love, your ring has no beginning and no end.
Family problems come, in sickness and health
Good times and bad through poverty and wealth
The ring on your finger wraps around your soul
Pride makes you strong, but love keeps you whole.
Feel the love from your ring, cherish it and smile
With affection, knowing it has all been worth while
Sparkling jewels and diamonds are all for pleasure
But your gold wedding band is to treasure forever.
As long carefree years of memories unfold
We take for granted this circle of gold
Throughout married life it has always been there
When you take your last breath and whisper a prayer
As your time on this earth sadly comes to an end
Your old wedding ring is your final friend.

Dying Time

Tentatively I walk into heavens waiting room
with opaque lights and soft plush furniture.
The grained wood doors remind me of coffins.
Serenity and calm splash from the walls
echoing hushed voices, conversation brief.
Emotional weariness scars the faces
as they wait.
This is the dying time.
I watch as unconsciousness comforts its captive,
releasing the inner child.
Pallid features hold an expression of leaving spent things.
Time is irrelevant
life in limbo, suspended.
As death, waits in the wings.

Depression

Negative thoughts bombard my tormented mind
provoking caustic pain. Unanswerable questions,
why do I feel like this? So lonely and alone
when love is all around me, a stranger inside myself.
I feel crushed by the weight of my feelings
In this dark place, as despair screams in my chest
choking with tears stuck in my throat.
I cannot throw off this blanket of worry that buries me,
smothering everything that matters,
as this premonition of impending doom
sharpens the Jagged edges of darkness,
ravaging the gentle lilt of life, lost in sadness.

The Last Straw

His gambling obsession had turned to aggression
the fact that she feared him kept him amused
trapped in loneliness and desperation
her tired young body, bruised and abused.
She knew the dinner had to be ready
nervously slicing his bread on the side
saucepans simmer steadily on the stove
dread filled her body as the door flung wide.
"Lost again!" she sighed, the bitter words were out
too late---he heard her, she feared his mood
angrily flying at her, she turned away
knowing too well his crude attitude.
"I'm sick of your sarcastic remarks!" He spat
dragging her arm over the pan of steam
"I didn't mean anything please!" She begged
holding her fast, with a terrified scream.
A volcano of hate erupted inside her
With the searing pain she spun her arm round
quickly knocking the pan all over him
as the screaming bully fell to the ground.
Carrying the boiling pans from the stove
she poured them over him, one at a time,
writhing in pain he begged her forgiveness
walking out calmly she dialled 999.

The House Upon the Hill

The sun was highest in the sky
I felt the heat upon my face,
I aimlessly wandered not knowing why
Until I found a faraway place.
It looked so peaceful I slowed my pace
A perfect haven my heart to fill,
Scented copse and woodland chase
I saw my house upon the hill.

Oh what a sight my heart doth cry
Thatching roof like woven lace,
This must be mine or I will die
Windows shine like jewelled mace
Bright coloured hues of flowers blaze
Daisy and primrose on the window sill
Climbing rose the wall doth grace
I saw my house upon the hill.

I saw humming bee and butter fly
All around the garden race
I cannot move although I try
With love my eyes embrace
The birds sing tenor and in bass
Sweet chorus sounds so trill
Stepping back my footsteps trace
I saw my house upon the hill.

Envoi....
Husband dear, I plead my case
Pray this will be thy will
To buy a dream is no disgrace
I saw my house upon the hill.

17

A Poem of Love

Our love has no barriers
Precious as time itself
I watch you breathe, deep and slow
and pray God will take me first.
There could be no life without you,
You are the core of my being,
I breathe you in.
My world is where you are
and when I am alone, I ache for your nearness.
How can you love me, with all my faults?
Our eyes play games together, and I am turned inside out.
You smile and the sun shines,
our hands touch, and I can fly.

The Allotment

This landscape of corrugated sheets, sheds and lean-to's
fill the skyline, with a slower pace of time
as urban traffic hums,
with plastic tubs and water butts
recycled doors, windows and old oil drums.
Leaning railings divide each allocated plot
forming a patchwork quilt of organised chaos, yet
on closer inspection sit regimental rows of runner beans on canes
growing to perfection.
Another section for potatoes
a mish mash collection of root vegetables
and orderly peas tied up with string.
Planted from seed with grubby hands and broken back
in an all-weather love affair with nature.
This fellowship of gardeners provides an organic feast
complete with slugs, sludge and caterpillar eggs
from this urban oasis.
Cockeyed paths between rows
Lead to window panes turned into cold frames
beside a ramshackle shed, where a shabby armchair
becomes a throne of contentment.
Surrounded by archaic tools and muddy boots, a flask of tea,
a quiet smoke, away from interfering folk.
This self sufficient world away from the stresses of modern life
a perfect hobby of solitude, without a nagging wife.

Working Class Woman

I've seen so much change happen over the years
cash in a pay packet soon disappears
then salaried monthly paid into a bank
with pensions and tax, the wages soon shrank.
Required to work shifts afternoons and nights
at last, equal pay and then women's rights
Union meetings working to rule
strike for full pay, we're nobody's fool.
Holidays with pay were soon introduced
we fought long and hard to stop sexual abuse
we voted for sick-pay, the minimum wage
with old fashioned management on the rampage.
I'm proud to think I've been part of this change
one voice in millions can have so much range
I used my voice wisely to shout out loud
Im a working class woman, honest and proud.

Regeneration

No more blackened earth
winding gear or slag heaps on the sky line.
Long gone remnants of our gritty heritage.
Of communities bound together with coal.
Wheels of power, blend into lush fields
of unceasing movement,
green and gold now cover the scars.
Nature reclaims what is rightfully hers,
a copse embellished with bluebells
a limpid stream murmuring
to wild garlic and celandine,
does it remember the murky past?
A warm wind blusters,
flinging itself around me
as I gorge greedily on the view,
a valley, reborn.

The Lemon

Hold a lemon and inhale a vision.
Rows of fragrant trees, lush green leaves
with branches profusely hung with lemons
ripening in the Mediterranean sun.
Grown in the heat, the colour of sunshine.
Slice into the citrus rind
and watch the pungent zest
squirt in to the air bursting like a roman candle.
Taste buds explode and eyes water as the
sourness of the piquant flesh reaches the tongue
as the mouth waters with the sharpness of its juice.
This versatile fruit has many uses
but my perfect joy is with ice,
in a glass of gin and tonic.

I Know

I know you love me.
from the moment I was born
you were there for me.
Our memories endless
though now so thoughtless.

I know you are sorry
yet never apologise,
why do you hurt me?
harsh words I try to ignore
gone, the man I knew before.

I know you so well
your selfishness pushes me
I can't walk away
from a love so demanding,
this silent understanding.

I know you have fears
what tomorrow may bring.
I do understand.
The anxious dread you measure
spoil times we should treasure.

I know you are old, but
time left a granite heart
with cold distant gaze.
Loneliness age can consume,
still your smile lights up the room.

Roadkill

Not the glorious death by the shotgun in
the game of skill between man and his prize.

His death should be instant, honourable
In his own habitat.

This proud game bird with cocky stance
a flamboyant beauty, now lies motionless.

His majestic head of bottle green, contrived
in the deep red stain on the gravel.

Feathers of rich browns tinged with gold,
still lustre moving with the wind.

Eyes glazed, he wears the death mask
expressionless in the gutter
as unconcerned traffic whizzes by.

Road Rage

I bought myself a little car, I've had it quite a while
and when I'm tootling down the road I always have to smile
for most the time I'm very good my driving skills top level
but when I put the seat belt on, I turn into a devil!
I'm usually quite mild mannered, a tantrum is somewhat rare
but if I'm upset behind the wheel I can't half curse and swear
I raise my middle digit so I'm not misunderstood
I shake my fist and honk the horn, my French is very good!
One day while stood at traffic lights In a quiet train of thought
as lights turned green from behind me came a screeching Volvo sport,
It shot straight in front of me which gave me quite a scare,
he just missed my wing, I had to swerve, this made my nostrils flare!
"You bleeping stupid idiot" I screamed "Are you insane?"
he just gave me the V-sign and tore off down the lane.
Well this man's rudeness on the road I found it hard to swallow
I then turned into a devil, so I knew I had to follow!
The Volvo sport shot off, just like a rocket down the road
my foot was flat down to the floor, I thought I would explode
he knew I was behind him, with my horn I gave a blast
I shook my fist and flashed the lights; I stuck there hard and fast
until we reached the village, he braked quickly with a lurch
behind a funeral cortege he stopped dead outside the church!

He jumped out of the Volvo sport my heart was beating quicker
my god I couldn't believe my eyes.... the driver was the vicar!
He marched, red faced towards me it was then I lost my bottle
I banged the car into reverse and pushed down on the throttle
I did the quickest three point turn and sped off at some pace
praying that the vicar hadn't recognised my face
but I had to go confess my sins again, at Sunday mass
with the vicar in the pulpit glaring down as bold as brass!
He was preaching 'Love thy neighbour' so all you sinners beware!"
he stared at me, I bowed my head and quietly said a prayer,
but after mass I shook his hand I didn't want to goad
then smiling, handed him a copy of the latest Highway Code!!!

Pain

You arrive unannounced from a dark place,
raising your ugly head.
 A demon possessing my body.
Screaming through the eye of the storm
and dashing me against the rocks.
Again and again you strike
piercing as a hot iron.
Craving attention, numbing my thoughts
controlling me.
Monster of destruction you return
to me like some horrific nightmare
filling me with dread,
dragging me through a tunnel of fear,
shutting out the light
as I lie, drenched in darkness, broken.
I pray that you will go,
get out of my life, leave me
and let me quickly close the door.

My Fat World

Nowadays its watch your weight and keep your body trim
Its low-fat milk and quinoa, then get down to the gym.

Exercise is what I need but it's so boring and not much fun
I'd rather sit and watch TV and enjoy a fresh cream bun.

Alcohol only in moderation, slim line tonic is good indeed
But it doesn't lift my spirits, when wine is what I need!

I'm sick to death of salads and lunch with low-fat spread
And if I eat one more Ryvita I'm taking to my bed!

I live with constant craving for pork pie or fish and chips
It's so unfair I enjoy the food that goes straight on my hips.

I've had enough of slimming soup and rock hard melba toast
I just need some Yorkshire puddings and a proper Sunday roast!

They say just eat whatever you like, but have a smaller plate
I do, but I'm still hungry, so I have a slice of cake.

They say lots of sex helps your diet, satisfaction is not guaranteed
But sex doesn't quite fit the bill, when a Mars bars what I need!

So to hell with bad cholesterol, I'll eat what's in front of my eyes
What's wrong with being fat and happy? I'll just buy a bigger size!

Women of War

Women of war did bravely endeavor
To change their way of life forever
With shovel and pick they mended the road
Lay the bricks and carried the load,
They ground the flour then baked the bread,
Dug the graves and buried the dead.
They drove the trucks, and changed the wheel
Made the shells, and forged the steel
Twilight falls and they stand at the gate,
Praying to god, and wait, and wait.

With dry eyes, they faced reality
Shocked to hear wars brutality
Saving their tears for their empty bed,
Dreading the heartaches that lie ahead.
They mourned together when hells horror came,
Knitting socks by a flickering flame.
In muddy trenches their brave men died
King and country to be justified,
Evening falls and they stand at the gate,
Praying to god, and wait, and wait.

The Front Line

They lie in filth
gaunt faces blurred
with blood and fear
groping for life.
Broken and beat
In tattered khaki
and rotting boots.
The boom of guns
flash in the sky.
Dazed for want of sleep
the battle weary
throb and ache,
spared from death
for one more night.
Silently they pray.
Cold drenching rain
soak dead men
in furrows of sorrow.
Gone is the glory
the blush of youth
blown away.
Death outnumbers life
In this hellhole.

Mrs. Bond

Why the hell do I stay, why should I care?
About a crazy man that disappears everywhere
He comes home scratched and bruised or worse
I've a hell of a job getting blood off his shirts,
I'm sick of repairing his suit that gets ripped
He thinks I don't notice his flies are unzipped.
Outside of Harrods I wait and I wait
then smelling of perfume the pig turns up late,
he ponces around in his new Aston Martin
while I put up with his belching and farting,
but the sex is great! Yes I have to admit
when he jumps off the wardrobe it helps me keep fit.
He wears his tuxedo just bursting with charm
I'm simply eye-candy that's linked on his arm
but I'm still his wife and I won't be deterred
he loves my martini which is shaken not stirred.
You may smile thinking Aaaahh just another dumb blonde,
But my name is Jane.... yes I'm Jane Bond!

Michelangelo and Me

We first met in Rome outside Vatican City
He looked a bit strange but was ever so witty
"Mi chiamo is signor Michelangelo"
The glint in his eye set my cheeks all aglow.
He bought some wine and we chatted all night
Turned out he was a painter, a bit of all right
That's handy I thought and I had to confess
I could do with a painter; my lounge is a mess.
We agreed on a price then I said goodbye
To be honest I thought I'd seen the last of the guy
But two weeks later he arrived on my step
He'd travelled to Manchester on Easy Jet.
He kissed me "Ciao" I smiled hiding my blushes
All he brought with him was a bagful of brushes!
So I took him shopping and we bought the paint
He made it quite clear there could be no constraint
He explained 'high renaissance' was his kind of style
Well I hadn't a clue so I went out for a while
When I returned, well I had a convulsion
I thought he would give it just a coat of emulsion!
But the ceiling and walls were completely transformed
Into a work of art with colours that warmed with
Naked cherubs cavorting all over the walls
That will be embarrassing when the vicar calls!

Frescos telling stories of prophets and angels with God
and Elvis in the centre, which I thought was quite odd
he was playing his guitar with a swivel on his hips
wearing blue suede shoes and that pout on his lips.
well I fell in love with his impassioned style
And my Italian stallion stayed for a while
But alas one day the Pope phoned him from Rome
with a job painting the chapel, so Michael flew home
but he left me his number so I'm patiently waiting
I'll give him a call when the kitchen needs painting.

The Land of Deliciousness

I fell off a rainbow, and lost my address
And woke up in a land called Deliciousness
I walked through fields of sugared flowers
Where cows had cream horns and pigs had showers.
Fish with fingers were swimming in the lake
And all the houses were made of fruit cake.
There were lots of babies all made of jelly
The moon was cream cheese, though not quite as smelly.
I sat beneath a toffee apple tree
With a sausage dog, and a nice cup of tea
Then buttered toast soldiers came marching by
They wore chocolate buttons, on thick crusty rye.
I asked a dandelion clock "What's the time?"
But all he could say was "Its lemon or lime."
I dined with a bee on the sweet honeycomb
Then climbed on his back, and the bee flew me home.

The La De Da Lady

A la de da lady came into the store
quite old I'd say, and dressed like a whore
"I need a new outfit and furthermore
it must flatter my hour glass figure
I'm a small 12!"
Well that made me snigger,
Anyone with eyes could see she was bigger.
So with a smile, into the aisle
I pulled out a rail full of garments with style.
When she went to undress I must confess
I knew this lady had no finesse.
"I can't do this zip, it's not right on my hip,
I don't wear a high waist, doesn't suit my face,
Is this the right size, it doesn't flatter my thighs!
this is no good it's off the shoulder,
I can't wear that colour, it makes me look older.
this is not to my taste; I don't like the lace
oh this is quite smart with the dogtooth check
what a shame, it's no good too high in the neck!"
By this time, I was a nervous wreck
too long too short too big too small
nothing could suit the lady at all,
she had tried every outfit we had in the shop
I was just about ready to blow my top.
Then to the rescue there came a co worker
on her way to the stockroom, she carried a Burqa
the la de da lady screamed in delight
"It's perfect it's perfect! That outfits just right,
but to match my shoes do you have it in white?"

The Ashes

My husband's in the wardrobe
I can't bear to say goodbyes
so he's there where I can see him
with all the suits and ties.
I placed him on the top shelf
beside the shirts without a crease
that belonged to my next husband
who sits on the mantelpiece.
My husband's in the garden
beside his favourite apple tree
he just collapsed in the cabbage patch
that was husband number three.
My husband's under the bed
his snoring would never cease
he snored so loud he choked to death
now I can rest in peace.
I've recently remarried
A young man from Guatemala
he's changed the name from "Home Sweet Home"
it's now the "Funeral Parlour."

My Boy

That's not my boy with hate in his eyes,
a pitiless monster I've learned to despise
I don't know this boy, wicked and tough
his life was his gang, we were never enough.
I courted false hope God knows how I tried,
his demons took over he stole and he lied.
My boy has gone I lost him to drugs,
cocaine and crack and mixing with thugs.
My boy was warm, thoughtful, and giving
his cheeky smile made it easy forgiving.
Too little good and too much bad
I grieve long and hard for the boy I once had.
I knew this would come when he carried a knife,
I told him and told him It would cost him his life,

But he took someone else's
another life ...
gone
another mother, now
grieves for her son.
that's not my boy,
his sentence now sworn,
take him away
and leave me, to mourn.

No Tomorrows

I see them, sat in chairs
not dead yet not alive
trapped inside the prison cell of old age
without thought of time or season.
People alien from the world
careless of dress, done with life.
No more watching the world go by
some have out worn their sins
as the joy of living grows further away
sleep comes as sweet relief
when there are no tomorrows.
Among the spectral faces
I glimpse a smile of wistfulness
lit up by memories golden rays
a kiss that once pressed my cheek.
Now I see a child behind those sad eyes
despondent weary and bowed
a broken spirit, no longer proud.

Decorating

Like a military operation
the room is prepared
stripped naked
laid bare.
Furniture shivers with cold
hidden under sheets.
The paste table stands proud
as battle weary steps creak to attention
manoeuvred carefully into position.
Each strip meticulously measured
matching carefully each flower petal
and stem with a snip.
Across the table the huge brush
smothers and slaps gloopy paste
from a sticky bucket.
Each precious piece caressed into position
with perfect precision
lovingly pressed and dabbed.
Stand back, check, and admire.
The room smiles,
and slowly comes back to life.

First Kiss

I remember well my first kiss
virgin lips on virgin lips
looking into nervous eyes
hot breath intensifies,
cold nose brushing my cheek
strange fluttering feeling weak
startled, broke away
couldn't find a thing to say
I remember clearly feeling glad,
but can't remember
the name of the lad!

Tinselled Winter

I rise to find a raw white morning.
Frost has painted the earth with brittle hands
scattering crystals of silver snow dust
transforming garden pavement and road
blanketing a mist of eerie silence.
Winters magic ages the landscape as
white whiskers form beneath a lacy shawl
of diamond droplets from tinselled branches.
The once-green grass has turned to frozen spears,
as cruel Winter waves its icy wand.

The Fallen

When an autumn breeze blows
Into a leaf strewn corner of England
we remember the blown away petals of history
In a faraway country....

They lie together in green fields
designed spaces geometric grids,
row upon row of white granite.
Precise uniformity patterned to our past
 as far as the eye can see
entombed in quiet openness,
 just names and numbers.
Flowers now squeeze through battled soil
the ground below is full of bones
of what used to be wide eyed young men
they had not learned of sorrow then
nor strife death or sad parting.
The graveyards full of deaths coldness
brittle bodies wrapped in courage
each mother's son a tale to tell
wondering why so many had to die so well.
As life's silent movie plays on
we thank them for freedom and sing the amen
with the slow beat of the drum....
We will remember them.

Just Nineteen

I wanted him home but they said he wouldn't keep
they brought him home an hour before the funeral.
The tiny oak coffin was carried carefully into the front room
through an uncomfortable silence.

I remember it was frilled with pure white silk
"Our Loved One" embroidered in blue across his chest.
A wax doll, with cherub lips and a half smile sleeping peacefully.
I didn't think I could cry anymore.

The house was filled with tea and sympathy
flowers and feeling out of place, in black hats
and coats smelling of mothballs. Whispers inform strangers
"Sometimes these things happen for the best"

They lowered the small box into the cruel earth
that was the first time I saw my husband cry
I wanted to scream, I was just nineteen
but had lived for a hundred years.

The Wine Glass

What joy a glass of wine can bring, warming comforting
lubrication, a social intercourse of relaxation. Sweet
velvet fuel of fascination. Euphoria follows
intoxication, but beware if not taken in
moderation heartache and tears
will come to pass as you
drink the demons from
the glass. Sparkling
white, Rose` or red
can bring you
joy, or put
you in
bed.
L
I
Q
U
I
D
T
E
M
p
T
A
T
I
O
N
OFSTIMULATIONANDSOPHISTICATION

The Beach

Like confetti scattered in a churchyard
they crammed onto the beach.
Basking in summer sunshine
grouped together, gorging, on sandy sandwiches
family size crisps and coke.
The aroma of fish and chips
Invades the nostrils
as the abundance of bare flesh
slowly bakes from pale pink to red.
A sluggish cloud crept heavily, nobody noticed.
First a spit then a spot
then faster spits that splatter the skin,
thunder muttered and rolled
turning heads in panic.
Fathers grab their young
From the water's edge,
While frantic mothers gather up belongings.
Down it came, a deluge
darkening the sand,
like frantic ants they exit the beach
to the safety of amusement arcades
and shop doorways.
Awnings sag overwhelmed,
with the sudden torrent
swamping gutters and grates.
Only drenched donkeys
stand, bedraggled heads bowed
on the deserted beach,
waiting..

Innocence

Long awaited Saturday night
The place to be, set free
Like a bird from a cage
In stiletto heels and mini skirt.
Spirited youths strut their stuff
With confident expectation
With slicked hair smoking cigarettes
Tight jeans, geared up to flirt.

Beyond the haze of diesel fumes
Waltzes, dodgems, and carousel
Girls scream with delight, hold on tight
Wild rides that shake and clatter
Hot dogs, donuts and candy floss
Smells that make your mouth water
Try your luck, for a coconut
win a goldfish, even better.

Never before such innocence
His inviting smile catches her eye
Walking on air with excitement
They hold hands, things won't be the same
With pop music blaring constantly
As lights flash and sirens wail
They sneak off behind a caravan
Never such innocence again.

I am still me

A single room,
a single bed
between empty days
and nothing nights
I am drenched in loneliness.
Inside my head
I still dance.
Life beautiful and wild
was trod by me.
I see his face
In the webbed shadow
If I stare long enough
at faded curtains.
Trapped in uncertainty
I wait,
time is not a friend
but I am still me.

Eggshells

Looking back
on the whole rigmarole
of courting and cavorting.
Love, honour, always obey.
Wet sex and endless passion
as mundane life ticked on.
Walking on air turned to walking on
eggshells as jealousy seeped in.
Hating his obsession with possession,
slowly the fire went out.
Love now hard and cold
useless
As the band of gold.

Not even a Statistic

As tedious traffic throbs
safe from the gropers and jokers of this world
he lies in his cardboard refuge,
as human ants rush by.
The squalid figure cowers like a whipped dog
and no one asks why?
A doper no hoper, huddled in a doorway
ignored
unknown
not even a statistic.
Neglected truth, here lies the proof.
An adolescent old man burnt out in his youth.
A lifetime shows on his face of despair
another sad victim of circumstance
and who is to care?
A life overlooked.
On the edge between hell and euphoria

one more shot to self destruct.

Listen Loudly

Low mist covers the valley
as thin drizzle quenches the sod.
Laughing water trickles,
from an open wound in the earth.

Listen loudly
to darting insects, humming in chorus
with the melodious bird song,
as tall grasses sway to the rhythm,
the sun spreads in all her glory.

Listen loudly
on a mattress of grass
touch a blue expanse of openness,
once again the flowers smile,
tempting the plumptious honey bee.

Listen loudly
As rays of slanting light, filter
through whispering foliage,
ducks scrawl onto a mirrored lake
diving through a dense cloud of midges.

Listen loudly,
hear the peace.

This place is not for me

This place is not for me
I don't want to be here
but I must.
Long white corridors
bright, light glares above me
faces smile,
strong reassuring hands.
Talking, cheery voices,
I know they are saying
Don't worry,
But these are not my friends
I don't want to listen,
Take me home.
This place is not for me
I don't want to be here
But I must.

A Villanelle for Peace

Curse man and his brutality
can we not feel the Blackman's pain?
Peace for the world is a mockery.

Still famine causes misery
Just to satisfy rich mans gain,
Curse man and his brutality.

We bear the curse of slavery
and time will never break the chain,
Peace for the world is a mockery.

Children starving in poverty,
Death and disease through mans disdain,
Curse man and his brutality.

Religion, war, hostility,
Streets run with blood, young men lie slain
Peace for the world is a mockery.

Cry shame on our complicity
Indifference is inhumane,
Curse man and his brutality,
Peace for the world is a mockery.